The *Hanuman Chalisa*

The *Hanuman Chalisa*

Translated by

VIKRAM SETH

SPEAKING
TIGER

SPEAKING TIGER BOOKS LLP
125A, Ground Floor, Shahpur Jat, near Asiad Village,
New Delhi 110049

First published by Speaking Tiger Books in 2024

Painting on page 5: *Hanuman Bearing the Mountaintop with Medicinal Herbs*, Rajasthan, ca. 1800, Collection of The Met, NY.

ISBN: 978-93-5447-859-8

10 9 8 7 6 5 4 3 2 1

Typeset in ArnhemFine by SŪRYA, New Delhi
Printed at Print Works, New Delhi

Introduction

The *Hanuman Chalisa* by Tulsidas is one of the best-known and best-loved poems in the world. Tens of millions of people can recite it by heart, and chant it daily, as well as in times singularly joyful or sorrowful—or when they feel the need for support or courage.

So too did Bhaskar, the precocious young mathematician in *A Suitable Boy* who, as a child, loved to participate in the annual Ramlila in Brahmpur in his role as a monkey warrior.

I did this translation more than ten years ago as a labour of love, but have only recently been persuaded to publish it. I hope that it will enable the *Hanuman Chalisa* to be enjoyed by those who cannot understand the Hindi or Awadhi of the 16th century.

The *Hanuman Chalisa* is a hymn to Hanuman in his many mythic roles: warrior, protector, remover of obstacles, teacher, devotee, adviser, bestower of good things, intercessor, friend, miracle worker, god.

It consists of 43 rhymed couplets: two dohas by way of introduction; 40 chaupais, which is why it is called a Chalisa or 'Fortyverser'; and one final doha by way of coda.

Each line of a doha has a first half of 13 beats (or 'matras'); then a pause (or 'caesura'); then a second half of 11 beats. Each line of a chaupai has 16 beats, divided 4 + 4 + 4 + 4. These beats themselves are attached to the syllables of the poem: broadly speaking, a syllable has either 1 or 2 beats, depending on the length of the vowel it contains and whether it is or is not followed by a conjunct consonant.

This translation includes a phonetic transliteration, but no notes.

I was at first tempted to add a few notes. These would have discussed the history of the poem; its basic structure and movement; references to the names and events mentioned within the poem; and (dear to the heart of a poet) a detailed analysis of the rhythm and prosody of the dohas and chaupais (including exceptions to the standard beat-count of syllables, as well as Tulsidas's lively syncopation across divisions within a line of his chaupais). But I eventually decided against this on the grounds that it would encumber a simple translation with too much by way of apparatus.

I did decide, however, in order to make the sound of the poem accessible to those who cannot read the Hindi text, to add a simple phonetic transliteration—one which uses no superscripts, subscripts, italicisations or diacritical marks. (1) The short vowels, long vowels and diphthongs are written as follows: a, aa, i, ee, u, oo, e, ai, o, au. Where two vowels sit next to each other within a word, they are separated by a hyphen. (2) The light nasalisation of a vowel is written: '(n)' (3) The retroflex letters are shown as the capital letters T, D and R in order to distinguish them from their dental equivalents. As is the case with Hindi, nothing else is capitalised.

The transliteration corresponds, letter by letter, to the Hindi text, with one exception. The short 'a' is omitted whenever it appears at the end of a line of poetry—or just before the central pause in a line from a doha. (For example, the very last syllable of the *Hanuman Chalisa* is pronounced 'bhoop', not 'bhoopa'.) This is consonant with standard Hindi recital practice.

I translated the *Hanuman Chalisa* using both rhythm and rhyme because I wanted to convey something of the incantatory pleasure of the original. In order to replicate the pulse of the original chaupais, I used, for the most part, so-called falling metres, i.e., trochaic or dactylic metres. This meant using rhymes that are, like those in the original, stressed on the last but one syllable (such as 'ocean' and 'devotion'). These so-called feminine rhymes are rare in English, and I hope that my restriction to such rhymes has not forced me to take too many liberties with Tulsidas's text.

Another constraint should be mentioned: it was not possible to recreate the wonderfully musical echoes and alliterations of the original, such as the repeated nasal vowels of the 23rd chaupai or the repeated retroflex sounds of the 36th chaupai.

At any rate, all this is just a means, however imperfect, of acquainting or re-acquainting people with a magical and joyful work, impressed in the memories and affections of millions, which encapsulates a whole culture in fewer than ninety lines.

I dedicate this translation to Bhaskar, who learned the poem before he was five, but who spent his fifties fighting the chauvinism and intolerance to which this and many other well-beloved religious texts and rituals have been put.

Nothing could be further from the humanity and inclusivity of the best of Hinduism than the self-aggrandisement and wilful cruelty of those who use the religion in which—in the lottery of life—they happen to be born, in order to attack or demean others.

May the *Hanuman Chalisa* continue to spread joy, expand imagination and give strength and solace to its many past and future readers.

श्री हनुमान चालीसा

The *Hanuman Chalisa*

Dohas

श्री गुरु चरन सरोज रज, निज मनु मुकुरु सुधारि ।
बरनउँ रघुबर बिमल जसु, जो दायकु फल चारि ॥

बुद्धिहीन तनु जानिके, सुमिरौं पवन कुमार ।
बल बुद्धि विद्या देहु मोहिं, हरहु कलेस बिकार ॥

shree guru charana saroja raj,
nija manu mukuru sudhaari
barana-u(n) raghubara bimala jasu,
jo daayaku phala chaari

buddhiheena tanu jaanike,
sumirau(n) pavana kumaar
bala buddhi vidyaa dehu mohi(n),
harahu kalesa bikaar

Having cleansed with the dust of my teacher's
feet the mirror of my mind and being,
I sing of Ram, from whom all things come:
truth, means, desire and freeing.

Knowing how shallow my learning is,
to you, Hanuman, I pray—
Grant to me wisdom, knowledge and strength;
take every blemish away.

Chaupais

जय हनुमान ज्ञान गुन सागर ।
जय कपीस तिहुँ लोक उजागर ॥१॥

jaya hanumaana gyaana guna saagar
jaya kapeesa tihu(n) loka ujaagar

1.

Hail Hanuman, great wisdom's ocean—
The three worlds glow with your light
and devotion.

रामदूत अतुलित बल धामा।
अंजनिपुत्र पवनसुत नामा ॥२॥

raamadoota atulita bala dhaamaa
anjaniputra pavanasuta naamaa

2.

Envoy of Ram, in mightiness towering;
Anjani's son, and the Wind's, overpowering.

महाबीर बिक्रम बजरंगी ।
कुमति निवार सुमति के संगी ॥३ ॥

mahaabeera bikrama bajarangee
kumati nivaara sumati ke sangee

3.

Sturdy-limbed and brave past telling,
Friend of the good, all evil dispelling,

कंचन बरन बिराज सुबेसा ।
कानन कुंडल कुंचित केसा ॥४॥

kanchana barana biraaja subesaa
kaanana kunDala kunchita kesaa

4.

Golden-bodied—in fine robes appearing,
Curly haired—on each side an earring,

हाथ बज्र औ ध्वजा बिराजै ।
काँधै मूँज जनेऊ साजै ॥५॥

haatha bajra au dhwajaa biraajai
kaa(n)dhe moo(n)ja jane-oo saajai

5.

Banner and mace raised before the beholder,
The sacred thread across your left shoulder,

संकर सुवन केसरीनंदन ।
तेज प्रताप महा जग बंदन ॥६॥

sankara suvana kesareenandan
teja prataapa mahaa jaga bandan

6.

Kesari's son and Shiva's descendant,
The world for its light upon you is dependent.

विद्यावान गुनी अति चातुर ।
राम काज करिबे को आतुर ॥७॥

vidyaavaana gunee ati chaatur
raama kaaja karibe ko aatur

7.

Deeply virtuous, wise and clever,
Eager to serve Lord Ram forever,

प्रभु चरित्र सुनिबे को रसिया।
राम लखन सीता मन बसिया ॥८॥

prabhu charitra sunibe ko rasiyaa
raama lakhana seetaa mana basiyaa

8.

Avid to hear his tale in the telling
—Ram, Lakshman, Sita
    within your heart dwelling—

सूक्ष्म रूप धरि सियहिं दिखावा ।
बिकट रूप धरि लंक जरावा ॥६॥

sookshma roopa dhari siyahi(n) dikhaawaa
bikaTa roopa dhari lanka jaraawaa

9.

Tiny in form—thus Sita discerning;
Awesome in form—setting Lanka burning;

भीम रूप धरि असुर सँहारे ।
रामचंद्र के काज सँवारे ॥१०॥

bheema roopa dhari asura sa(n)haare
raamachandra ke kaaja sa(n)waare

10.

Fierce-formed like Bhim—
    the demon-horde slaying;
Act after act, Lord Ram obeying.

लाय सजीवन लखन जियाये ।
श्री रघुबीर हरषि उर लाये ॥११॥

laaya sajeevana lakhana jiyaaye
shree raghubeera harashi ura laaye

11.

You brought the herb
    that was Lakshman's salvation;
Ram pressed you close
    to his heart with elation.

रघुपति कीन्ही बहुत बड़ाई ।
तुम मम प्रिय भरतहि सम भाई ॥१२॥

raghupati keenhee bahuta baRaa-ee
tuma mama priya bharatahi sama bhaa-ee

12.

Praising your virtues one after another:
'You are as dear as is Bharat, my brother.

सहस बदन तुम्हरो जस गावैं।
अस कहि श्रीपति कंठ लगावैं ॥१३॥

sahasa badana tumharo jasa gaawai(n)
asa kahi shreepati kanTha lagaawai(n)

13.

Voice after voice
    sings your praise and adores you.'
Ram, with these words,
    to his bosom now draws you.

सनकादिक ब्रह्मादि मुनीसा ।
नारद सारद सहित अहीसा ॥१४॥

sanakaadika brahmaadi muneesaa
naarada saarada sahita aheesaa

14.

Brahma, Shesh, Narad—the four Sanak sages—
Hermits—Saraswati—saints down the ages—

जम कुबेर दिगपाल जहाँ ते ।
कबि कोबिद कहि सके कहाँ ते ॥१५॥

jama kubera digapaala jahaa(n) te
kabi kobida kahi sake kahaa(n) te

15.

Yama, Kuber and the heavens' guards
 praise you;
Can a mere poet presume to upraise you?

तुम उपकार सुग्रीवहिं कीन्हा ।
राम मिलाय राजपद दीन्हा ॥१६॥

tuma upakaara sugreevahi(n) keenhaa
raama milaaya raajapada deenhaa

16.

Through you, Sugriva, whom fate had mistreated,
Met Ram, and thus on his throne was re-seated.

तुम्हरो मंत्र बिभीषन माना ।
लंकेस्वर भए सब जग जाना ॥१७॥

tumharo mantra bibheeshana maanaa
lankeswara bhaye saba jaga jaanaa

17.

Through your advice was Vibhishan invested
Lanka's great king, as the world has attested.

जुग सहस्र जोजन पर भानू ।
लील्यो ताहि मधुर फल जानू ॥१८॥

juga sahasra jojana para bhaanoo
leelyo taahi madhura phala jaanoo

18.

Far in the distance, the Sun burned so brightly.
Like a sweet fruit, you just swallowed it lightly.

प्रभु मुद्रिका मेलि मुख माहीं ।
जलधि लाँघि गए अचरज नाहीं ॥१६॥

prabhu mudrikaa meli mukha maahee(n)
jaladhi laa(n)ghi gaye acharaja naahee(n)

19.

Ram's ring in your mouth,
    you leapt over the ocean!
Who'd be surprised
    by your strength and devotion?

दुर्गम काज जगत के जेते ।
सुगम अनुग्रह तुम्हरे तेते ॥२०॥

durgama kaaja jagata ke jete
sugama anugraha tumhare tete

20.

All the world's tasks, so confused and contorted,
Thanks to your grace, are untangled and sorted.

राम दुआरे तुम रखवारे ।
होत न आज्ञा बिनु पैसारे ॥२१॥

raama du-aare tuma rakhawaare
hota na aagyaa binu paisaare

21.

Outside Ram's door, it is you who stands sentry.
No one, without your permission, gains entry.

सब सुख लहै तुम्हारी सरना ।
तुम रक्षक काहू को डरना ॥२२॥

saba sukha lahai tumhaaree saranaa
tuma rakshaka kaahoo ko Daranaa

22.

Thanks to your grace, joy is born
    and is heightened.
You're here to save us; why then be frightened?

आपन तेज सम्हारो आपै ।
तीनों लोक हाँक तें काँपै ॥२३॥

aapana teja samhaaro aapai
teeno(n) loka haa(n)ka te(n) kaa(n)pai

23.

You alone can control your own fire;
The three worlds quake
    when you roar out your ire.

भूत पिसाच निकट नहिं आवै ।
महाबीर जब नाम सुनावै ॥२४॥

bhoota pisaacha nikaTa nahi(n) aawai
mahaabeera jaba naama sunaawai

24.

Those who recite your name and your merit
Fend off every ghost and malevolent spirit.

नासै रोग हरै सब पीरा ।
जपत निरंतर हनुमत बीरा ॥२५॥

naasai roga harai saba peeraa
japata nirantara hanumata beeraa

25.

Those whose tongues your glory borrow
Ward off all disease and sorrow.

संकट तें हनुमान छुड़ावै ।
मन क्रम बचन ध्यान जो लावै ॥२६॥

sankaTa te(n) hanumaana chhuRaawai
mana krama bachana dhyaana jo laawai

26.

Those whose deeds, words, meditation
Dwell on you, you grant salvation.

सब पर राम तपस्वी राजा ।
तिन के काज सकल तुम साजा ॥२७॥

saba para raama tapaswee raajaa
tina ke kaaja sakala tuma saajaa

27.

Ram, the sage king, reigns serenely.
All his tasks, you handle keenly.

और मनोरथ जो कोइ लावै ।
सोइ अमित जीवन फल पावै ॥२८॥

aura manoratha jo ko-i laawai
so-i amita jeevana phala paawai

28.

Those who tell you their longings purely
Gain life's deathless fruits securely.

चारों जुग परताप तुम्हारा ।
है परसिद्ध जगत उजियारा ॥२६॥

chaaro(n) juga parataapa tumhaaraa
hai parasiddha jagata ujiyaaraa

29.

All four ages resound with your story;
Through the whole world
    spread the rays of your glory.

साधु संत के तुम रखवारे ।
असुर निकंदन राम दुलारे ॥३०॥

saadhu santa ke tuma rakhawaare
asura nikandana raama dulaare

30.

Saints' and sages' guardian pillar,
Ram's beloved, demon killer!

अष्ट सिद्धि नौ निधि के दाता ।
अस बर दीन जानकी माता ॥३१॥

ashTa siddhi nau nidhi ke daataa
asa bara deena jaanakee maataa

31.

Nine great gifts, eight yogic powers—
Grant us the boons that Sita showers.

राम रसायन तुम्हरे पासा ।
सदा रहो रघुपति के दासा ॥३२॥

raama rasaayana tumhare paasaa
sadaa raho raghupati ke daasaa

32.

In Ram's essence deep and fervent
Ever remain his faithful servant.

तुम्हरे भजन राम को पावै ।
जनम जनम के दुख बिसरावै ॥३३ ॥

tumhare bhajana raama ko paawai
janama janama ke dukha bisaraawai

33.

Through your hymns we receive Ram's kernel,
Freed from rebirth's griefs eternal.

अन्तकाल रघुबर पुर जाई ।
जहाँ जन्म हरिभक्त कहाई ॥३४ ॥

antakaala raghubara pura jaa-ee
jahaa(n) janma haribhakta kahaa-ee

34.

Death will guide us to Ram's dwelling—
As devotees born, all doubt dispelling.

और देवता चित्त न धरई ।
हनुमत सेइ सर्ब सुख करई ॥३५॥

aura devataa chitta na dhara-ee
hanumata se-i sarba sukha kara-ee

35.

Don't let other gods entice you.
Hanuman should quite suffice you!

संकट कटै मिटै सब पीरा।
जो सुमिरै हनुमत बलबीरा ॥३६॥

sankaTa kaTai miTai saba peeraa
jo sumirai hanumata balabeera

36.

For those who seek him through meditation,
Grief gives relief, pain liberation.

जय जय जय हनुमान गोसाईं ।
कृपा करहु गुरुदेव की नाईं ॥३७॥

jaya jaya jaya hanumaana gosaa-ee(n)
kripaa karahu gurudeva kee naa-ee(n)

37.

Hail, hail, hail—Hanuman, great teacher—
Bless me, O Lord, your humble beseecher.

जो सत बार पाठ कर कोई ।
छूटहि बंदि महा सुख होई ॥३८॥

jo sata baara paaTha kara ko-ee
chhooTahi bandi mahaa sukha ho-ee

38.

A hundred times who repeats this recital,
Freed from all bonds, will receive joy's requital.

जो यह पढ़ै हनुमान चालीसा ।
होय सिद्धि साखी गौरीसा ॥३६॥

jo yaha paRhai hanumaana chaaleesaa
hoya siddhi saakhee gaureesaa

39.

Chanting Hanuman's forty verses,
As Shiva attests, success disburses.

तुलसीदास सदा हरि चेरा ।
कीजै नाथ हृदय मँह डेरा ॥४०॥

tulaseedaasa sadaa hari cheraa
keejai naatha hridaya maha(n) Deraa

40.

Tulsidas, who will always serve you,
Prays, O Lord, in his heart to preserve you.

Doha

पवनतनय संकट हरन, मंगल मूरति रूप।
राम लखन सीता सहित, हृदय बसहु सुर भूप॥

pavanatanaya sankaTa haran, mangala
moorati roop
raama lakhana seetaa sahit, hridaya basahu
sura bhoop

Son of the Wind, crisis dispeller,
  blessed form, I implore—
With Ram, Lakshman and Sita,
  dwell thou in my heart's core.